The Best Tales Ever Told
GODS & GIANTS

Written by Stewart Ross
Illustrated by Francis Phillipps

COPPER BEECH BOOKS
BROOKFIELD, CONNECTICUT

© Aladdin Books Ltd 1997
© U.S. text 1997
Designed and produced by
Aladdin Books Ltd
28 Percy Street
London W1P 0LD

First published in
the United States in 1997 by
Copper Beech Books,
an imprint of
The Millbrook Press
2 Old New Milford Road
Brookfield, Connecticut 06804

Editor
Jim Pipe
Designed by
David West Children's Books
Designer
Simon Morse
Illustrated by
Francis Phillipps
Additional illustrations by
Ken Stott
– B.L. Kearley
Language Consultant
Matthew Townend

Printed in Belgium
Library of Congress
Cataloging-in-Publication Data
Ross, Stewart.
Gods and Giants : myths of
Northern Europe /
by Stewart Ross ; illustrated by
Francis Phillipps.
p. cm. — (The best tales ever told)
Includes index.
ISBN 0-7613-0706-0 (lib. bdg.)
1. Mythology, European—
Juvenile literature. 2. Legends—
Europe, Northern—Juvenile
literature. 3. Tales, Medieval.
I. Phillipps, Francis. II. Title.
III. Series.
BL980.E853R67 1997 97-19218
398.2'094—dc21   CIP AC

CONTENTS

INTRODUCTION

THIS IS A COLLECTION of some of medieval Europe's most famous and best-loved stories. They come from all over the continent, from snowy Russia in the north to sunny Spain in the south. Most of the tales have been told time and again in many languages. For example, the Italian story of *Romeo and Juliet* was made famous by the English playwright William Shakespeare.

Some tales, such as the Viking and Celtic myths of gods and giants (*bottom*) and the adventures of Don Quixote (*right*), were entirely made up. Other stories, known as legends, were based on real people and real events. King Arthur and Saint George actually existed, although they lived a long time before the time of the knights in armor.

People told stories for fun and to make sense of things they didn't understand. Thor, for example, explained the frightening noise of thunder. Many of the tales also had a moral – they were meant to teach people how to behave. The story of Robin Hood made it clear that poor people are often kinder than rich people.

All these stories have changed a lot over the centuries. To help you, we have picked out the best parts and made them easy to understand. That way, we hope you'll enjoy them as much as those who first heard them long ago.

A Guide to Tongue-Twisting
Some old names can be difficult to say. To make it easier for you, we have broken down all long names into words that you can recognize.

For example, Cuchulain should be said "coo-<u>kull</u>-in." The underlining is to show you where to say the word louder. So with Cuchulain, say the <u>kull</u> a bit louder than the coo and the in!

MERLIN'S MAGIC

THE DEVIL (or "Satan" to his friends) was fed up. So many Britons were becoming Christians, he thought he soon wouldn't have any followers left. What he needed was a devil child to manage his dirty work in Britain.

Choosing a young lady about to have a baby, he ordered his sprites to zero in the minute the child was born and make it really devilish. The woman felt something odd was happening in her tummy and, luckily for Britain, had a word with the local holy man. When she gave birth, he got to the child first and christened it Merlin. The sprites buzzed slowly back to hell with their tails between their legs.

It was clear from the start that Merlin was no ordinary boy. He didn't need diapers and chatted away in his crib so cleverly that his mother didn't have any idea what he was talking about. He knew magic without being taught and could even tell what was going to happen in the future.

The local king, Uther (<u>oo</u>-*thurr*) Pendragon, got to hear about Merlin, the magic child, and kept a close eye on him. Magicians could be very useful at court, so as soon as he grew up, Uther made Merlin his chief advisor.

The Wandering Poet
The real Merlin was a wandering Welsh poet who lived about 1,500 years ago. He was said to be able to look into the future. But when his king was defeated in battle, he went mad and fled deep into a forest, where he lived like a wild man.

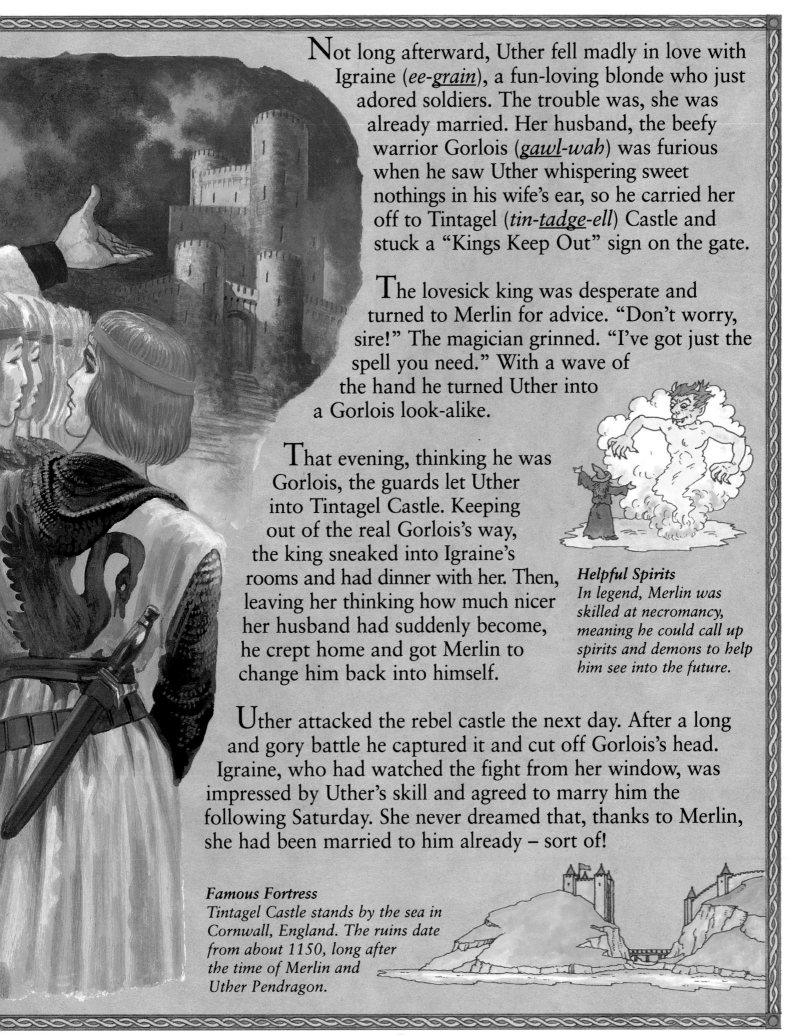

Not long afterward, Uther fell madly in love with Igraine (*ee-grain*), a fun-loving blonde who just adored soldiers. The trouble was, she was already married. Her husband, the beefy warrior Gorlois (*gawl-wah*) was furious when he saw Uther whispering sweet nothings in his wife's ear, so he carried her off to Tintagel (*tin-tadge-ell*) Castle and stuck a "Kings Keep Out" sign on the gate.

The lovesick king was desperate and turned to Merlin for advice. "Don't worry, sire!" The magician grinned. "I've got just the spell you need." With a wave of the hand he turned Uther into a Gorlois look-alike.

That evening, thinking he was Gorlois, the guards let Uther into Tintagel Castle. Keeping out of the real Gorlois's way, the king sneaked into Igraine's rooms and had dinner with her. Then, leaving her thinking how much nicer her husband had suddenly become, he crept home and got Merlin to change him back into himself.

Helpful Spirits
In legend, Merlin was skilled at necromancy, meaning he could call up spirits and demons to help him see into the future.

Uther attacked the rebel castle the next day. After a long and gory battle he captured it and cut off Gorlois's head. Igraine, who had watched the fight from her window, was impressed by Uther's skill and agreed to marry him the following Saturday. She never dreamed that, thanks to Merlin, she had been married to him already – sort of!

Famous Fortress
Tintagel Castle stands by the sea in Cornwall, England. The ruins date from about 1150, long after the time of Merlin and Uther Pendragon.

The SWORD in the STONE

The Real King Arthur lived long before the time of knights in armor. He was a half-Roman, half-British commander who fought against Anglo-Saxons.

Queen Igraine, wife of King Uther Pendragon, had a son named Arthur. Most people thought Arthur's father was the queen's first husband, so they didn't take much notice of the boy. Only Uther and Merlin, the magician, knew he was really the king's son, but they kept quiet.

Merlin now disappeared into the mountains of Wales to brush up on his magic. Shortly afterward Uther was poisoned, and fighting broke out to see who'd be the next king. For many years the kingdom dripped with blood, sweat, and tears.

When things were at their bloodiest and sweatiest, Merlin came back and went straight to the archbishop to ask him to hold a special service. Hundreds of knights turned up to see what Merlin was up to, filling the cathedral and overflowing onto the grass outside.

Just as the archbishop was beginning his sermon, a knight rushed into the cathedral yelling, "Amazing! A dirty great lump of marble with an anvil on top has landed in the churchyard! Lucky it didn't squash anyone!" The archbishop folded up his notes and went outside with everyone else to have a look.

There stood the anvil on its marble base. A sword was sticking out of the anvil, and a message around the base read: "He who pulls the sword out of the anvil is the king of Britain." The knights formed a line and took turns to have a heave.

The Court of King Arthur
King Arthur held his court at Camelot. This may have been the ancient fort of Cadbury in Somerset, England.

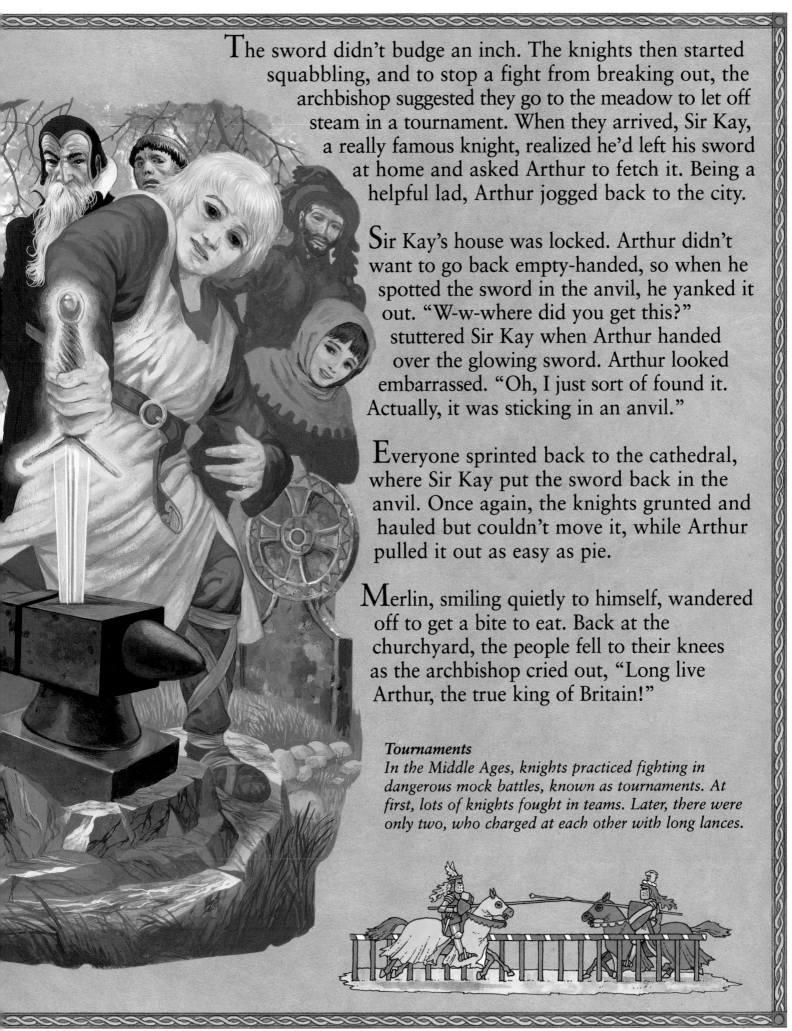

The sword didn't budge an inch. The knights then started squabbling, and to stop a fight from breaking out, the archbishop suggested they go to the meadow to let off steam in a tournament. When they arrived, Sir Kay, a really famous knight, realized he'd left his sword at home and asked Arthur to fetch it. Being a helpful lad, Arthur jogged back to the city.

Sir Kay's house was locked. Arthur didn't want to go back empty-handed, so when he spotted the sword in the anvil, he yanked it out. "W-w-where did you get this?" stuttered Sir Kay when Arthur handed over the glowing sword. Arthur looked embarrassed. "Oh, I just sort of found it. Actually, it was sticking in an anvil."

Everyone sprinted back to the cathedral, where Sir Kay put the sword back in the anvil. Once again, the knights grunted and hauled but couldn't move it, while Arthur pulled it out as easy as pie.

Merlin, smiling quietly to himself, wandered off to get a bite to eat. Back at the churchyard, the people fell to their knees as the archbishop cried out, "Long live Arthur, the true king of Britain!"

Tournaments
In the Middle Ages, knights practiced fighting in dangerous mock battles, known as tournaments. At first, lots of knights fought in teams. Later, there were only two, who charged at each other with long lances.

The BEST FIGHTER in IRELAND

EVERY BACHELOR IN IRELAND dreamed about Emer Forgall, the girl who looked like a supermodel and spoke like an actress. She was brainy, too, and never messed with strange men. But she was a bit choosy and refused to marry anyone who wasn't perfect.

Way to Go!
To the Celtic people of northwest Europe, the chariot was not just a way of getting around. It was also a fighting machine and a way of showing how important you were.

Teenage hero Cuchulain (*coo-kull-in*) reckoned he was just the sort of guy Emer was waiting for. He was clever, strong, and a really good warrior. The only trouble was his age – when he proposed to her she laughed and said she didn't fancy living with a schoolkid. He was really upset. "I can't help being younger than you," he cried. "Anyway, I bet you'd marry me if I was the best fighter in Ireland."

With this Ring
The custom of wedding rings goes back to ancient Egypt. It was worn on the third finger as this was supposed to have a vein leading straight to the heart.

Emer looked him over and said, "OK, Cuchulain. You prove you're the best fighter in Ireland *and* get me away from my family – and I'll marry you!" "It's a deal!" He grinned, and jumping into his chariot went charging off to tell his friends.

Mr. Forgall got mad as a hornet when he heard of the deal. He wanted his daughter to marry a prince, not some local bighead. So he went down to the pub and told his friends that the boy could prove he was the best fighter in Ireland by going to the Wild Woman and learning her battle skills. If he managed that, he'd have no trouble carrying off Emer, either.

No one had ever visited the Wild Woman and lived. But as Mr. Forgall hoped, when Cuchulain learned of the challenge he set off at once.

The path to her den lay across Bad-Luck Plain, through Dangerous Valley, and over Cliff Bridge. But the young hero got there with only a few scratches. Finding the Wild Woman asleep, he grabbed her by the hair and threatened to beat her up if she didn't tell him her fighting secrets. She didn't like wearing false teeth, so she agreed. The lad's neighbors were amazed when he came home in one piece, and they told Mr. Forgall he had certainly proved himself the best fighter in the land.

Do You Love Me?
Men and women have all kinds of strange ways of showing their love. Cuchulain did it by fighting. The women of the Tobriand Isles in the Pacific do it by biting the man they love!

Boudicca, the Fighting Queen
The most famous Celtic woman warrior was Boudicca (boo-dick-ah), Queen of the Icenii tribe, who led the British in a massive revolt against the Romans.

Now all Cuchulain had to do was rescue Emer. He zoomed around to her dad's castle in his chariot and vaulted right over the walls. Although the Forgalls fought like crazy, they were no match for the best fighter in Ireland, and half an hour later Cuchulain was roaring home again with Emer at his side.

The couple were married the following Saturday. That evening, after a few drinks, even old Mr. Forgall agreed that Cuchulain and Emer made a perfect pair.

ROBIN HOOD, *the* CHAMPION

"AN ARCHERY CONTEST, GUY?" sneered the sheriff of Nottingham. He had always thought that Guy of Gisborne was a bit of a softy.

"It might kill two birds with one stone, sire," Guy said nervously.

"Birds?" groaned the sheriff. "I want to kill outlaws, not birds!"

Guy explained how the contest would prove the sheriff's men were the best shots in the county, and if the outlaw Robin Hood turned up, they could arrest him the moment he showed his face. The sheriff smiled. It was, he agreed, rather a good plan after all.

The following Sunday, a huge crowd poured into the castle meadow to watch the competition. Sixty-three archers entered, but the sheriff was disappointed to learn that Robin Hood, who didn't often miss a chance to show off, wasn't among them.

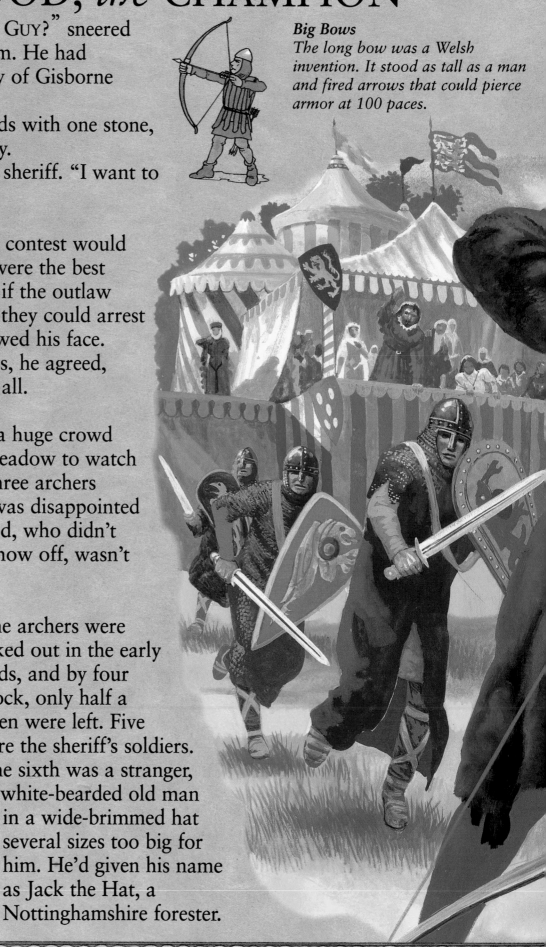

Big Bows
The long bow was a Welsh invention. It stood as tall as a man and fired arrows that could pierce armor at 100 paces.

Most of the archers were knocked out in the early rounds, and by four o'clock, only half a dozen were left. Five were the sheriff's soldiers. The sixth was a stranger, a white-bearded old man in a wide-brimmed hat several sizes too big for him. He'd given his name as Jack the Hat, a Nottinghamshire forester.

The Real Robin
The real Robin Hood probably lived in Yorkshire, England. He wasn't much of a hero because he robbed the rich and the poor alike!

After the next round only Jack and Clifton, the sheriff's top shot, were still in. Sure his man would win, the sheriff ordered a staff to be stuck in the ground 150 paces away. "A bag of gold if you hit it!" he cried.

Clifton fired first. His arrow hissed through the air and, to the crowd's amazement, thudded into the staff. "The winner!" cried the sheriff.

"Excuse me, sire," squeaked Jack the Hat, "but may I have my turn?"

The sheriff sighed. "OK, old man, but hurry up – Clifton wants his gold!"

Jack took careful aim. He had a very steady hand for a man of his age, the sheriff noticed. The bow twanged, and seconds later the crowd roared, "he's won! he's won!" Jack's arrow had split Clifton's down the middle!

"Take off your hat, fool!" the sheriff barked as Jack shuffled forward to collect his prize. When he hesitated, the sheriff leaned forward and knocked it to the ground. Long fair hair fell to the archer's shoulders. Off came the false beard, too – and there, grinning from ear to ear, stood Robin Hood, the outlaw!

The King's Deer
European kings of the Middle Ages had very strict laws to stop ordinary people hunting in their forests. The punishment for poaching (which Robin Hood did all the time) was death.

"Seize him!" shouted the sheriff. But Robin was too quick. Grabbing the gold and scattering it into the air, he vanished into the crowd. Minutes later he was safely back in the forest, laughing with his Merry Men about how he'd outwitted the sheriff of Nottingham yet again.

GEORGE *and the* DRAGON

Dragons were lazy beasts. After enjoying an excellent meal somewhere, rather than look for a new feeding ground, they always came back to the same place for more. The people of Joppa learned this at their cost.

One summer, a passing dragon swooped down on their fair and chewed up the mayor just as he was crowning the beauty queen. He was so fat and juicy that the monster came back the next week, and this time gobbled up the mayor's wife. After more flying visits, the citizens worked out a cunning antidragon plan.

Real Dragons
Some people think the idea of a dragon came from giant crocodiles. They can't fly or breathe fire, but they certainly eat people!

They held a weekly lottery. The winners got loads of money, but they had to give it to their families because they were taken outside the town and left tied to a stake as fast food for the dragon. Finding a regular supply of victims all trussed up and ready to eat, the beast left the town alone.

In mid-September, the beauty queen's mom foolishly bought her daughter a lottery ticket – and the poor girl won! The Joppans didn't like the idea of sacrificing her and she wasn't too happy, either. "There's not enough meat on me!" she wailed. But the rules were the rules, and she was tied to the stake ready for the dragon.

The fiery flapper appeared late that afternoon. Seeing the dainty morsel down below, he licked his scaly lips and got ready to land. The girl wriggled, screamed, and begged for mercy, but in the dragon's eyes this only made her more tempting. Great drops of saliva fell like rain from his gory jaws.

Fighting for God
The best knights in the Middle Ages followed the idea of chivalry. This meant being a good Christian and helping the weak against the wicked.

Roman George
The real St. George was not a knight in armor but a Roman soldier who was killed for being a Christian in about 300 A.D.

In those days Christian knights in armor made a habit of riding around the country looking for valiant deeds to perform. They got top honors for rescuing maidens in distress. As chance would have it, at that moment one of these wandering boy scouts clattered by and, hearing the girl's screams, he rode up to see what was going on.

Summing up the situation in an instant, he charged the dragon and skewered it in the belly with his lance. The monster roared with pain and spat a jet of flame straight at him. The knight, whose name was George, sheltered behind his shield and moved in for the kill. He stabbed and sliced and then, with one mighty blow, cut off the dragon's head.

Joppa was saved! So was the beauty queen, who had fallen madly in love with her brave rescuer and married him at once. She was not his only reward, either. The Joppans became Christians and George was made a saint.

Holy Helper
St. George became popular in England because in about 1098 he was supposed to have come to the rescue of some English soldiers fighting in the Middle East.

13

THOR'S WEDDING

THE VIKING GOD THOR was pretty handy with swords and spears, but his favorite weapon was a huge, club-shaped hammer known as Mjolnir (*me-earl-neer*). There was nothing he liked better than taking Mjolnir off to the mountains for a weekend of giant-bashing.

The Thunder God
Thor crashed around in a chariot pulled by a pair of gigantic goats, Toothgrinder and Toothgnasher. To the Vikings, thunder was the sound of his hammering, or the noise of kettles clattering around in the back of his chariot!

The dim-witted giants hated Thor's hammer thumpings. They also longed for someone to make the beds, cook the meals, and clean up around their cave. So, putting two and two together, they came up with a plan. One winter evening, when Thor was dozing beside the fire, a light-fingered giant crept into his house and carried Mjolnir off.

The next morning, after Thor had been up all night looking for his hammer, a raven flew in with a message from the mountains. The giants would give Mjolnir back, he croaked, if Thor got the love goddess, Freya (*fray-yah*), to marry the giants' king. Fingers crossed, Thor went over to Freya's to see what she thought of this idea.

"Marry a giant?" she yelled. "You must be crazy!" "Please," begged Thor. "After all, he is a king. And it's the only way I can get my Mjolnir back." Freya shook her head. "No way, Thor. If you want your precious hammer that badly, marry him yourself!"

OK, thought Thor, that's just what I will do! He found a wedding dress and pieces of jewelry in the gods' closet, wiped some makeup on his face, and set off for the mountains.

"What are you?" grunted the giants' guard when he saw the odd-looking visitor.

"I'm Freya, the love goddess," Thor squeaked, trying hard to look sexy. "I've come to marry your king." "Yum, yum!" muttered the guard, and ran off to tell his boss.

Most of the giants had never seen a woman before and they thought Thor was gorgeous. Even the king was pleased. "Mine!" he gurgled happily. "Pretty little wife, all mine!"

He went on grinning all through the wedding feast, even though Thor forgot himself and ate an ox and eight salmon, washed down with three barrels of mead. After the meal, the king said proudly to his bride, "Look, look at the lovely thing we stole!" He unwrapped Mjolnir from a red spotted handkerchief and handed it to Thor.

This was just what the god hoped would happen. He ripped off his dress and gave the giants such a hammering that they moved out of the mountains and were never seen again. But from this time onward, Thor always slept with Mjolnir tucked into his belt – just in case.

The Messenger of Doom
The black-plumed raven, which ate the flesh of dead animals, was feared as a sign of bad luck. In Ireland, ravens were trained to "talk." If one croaked "Bach," it meant that the next visitor would be a monk!

The END of the WORLD

THE PEOPLE OF THE NORTH were a gloomy bunch. They liked nothing better than sitting around in smoky halls chatting about the end of the world. They figured out exactly how it would happen, too, and their story goes something like this...

Things will start to fall apart when a spear of mistletoe pierces the heart of the noble Balder (*bal-dur*), Odin's second son. His body and soul are then taken off down to hell, the prison of death. The killing looks like an accident, but it isn't. It has been planned by a gang of villains who want to wipe out the gods.

Trickster God
Christians thought that he was the devil, but Loki was usually more of a trickster than a terror. He could change himself into any shape he wanted – a bird, a fish, or even a flea!

The gang is led by Loki (*lock-ee*), the "mischief maker" and father of all lies. When in a really bad mood, he can change himself into the blazing hot god of wildfire. He has three disgusting kids, who make up the rest of the gang. There is a gigantic wolf, a scaly sea serpent with ship-sized jaws, and Queen Hel, the wicked, green-eyed guard of the prison of death. The terrible trio are not a pretty sight.

After Balder's murder, the good gods realize Loki is getting too big for his evil boots, so they arrest him and chain him up. But they're too late. Loki feels in his rotten bones that the Old World can't last much longer and this gives him the muscles of a million whales.

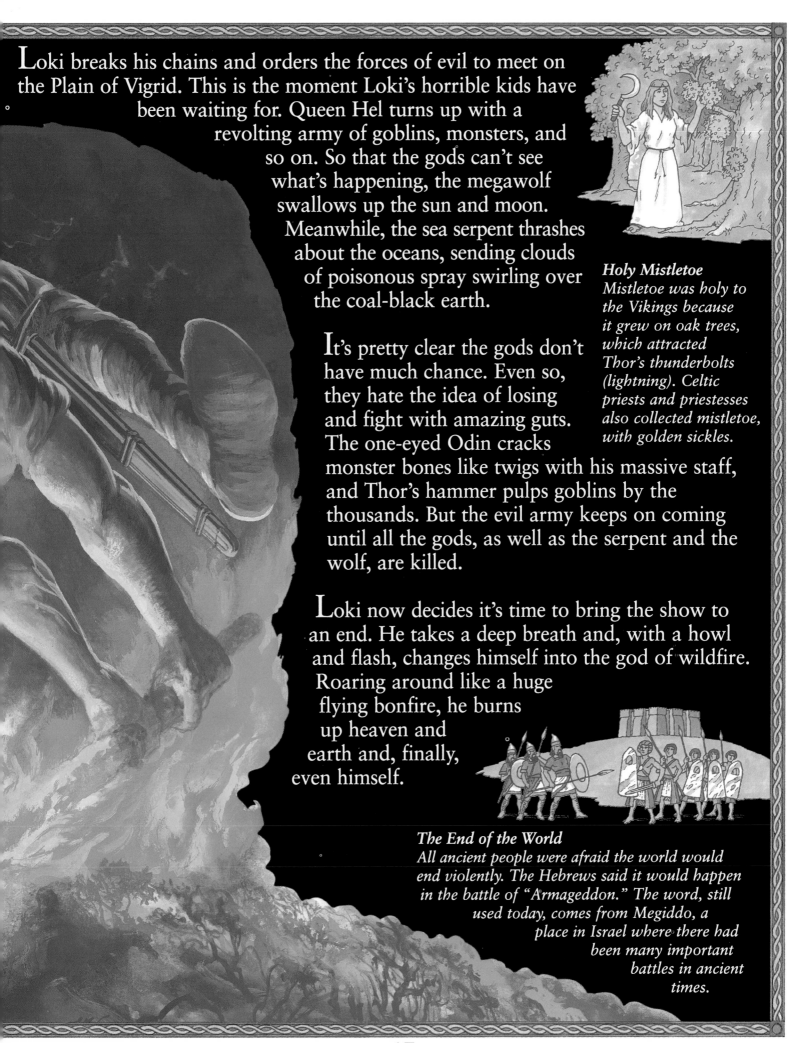

Loki breaks his chains and orders the forces of evil to meet on the Plain of Vigrid. This is the moment Loki's horrible kids have been waiting for. Queen Hel turns up with a revolting army of goblins, monsters, and so on. So that the gods can't see what's happening, the megawolf swallows up the sun and moon. Meanwhile, the sea serpent thrashes about the oceans, sending clouds of poisonous spray swirling over the coal-black earth.

It's pretty clear the gods don't have much chance. Even so, they hate the idea of losing and fight with amazing guts. The one-eyed Odin cracks monster bones like twigs with his massive staff, and Thor's hammer pulps goblins by the thousands. But the evil army keeps on coming until all the gods, as well as the serpent and the wolf, are killed.

Loki now decides it's time to bring the show to an end. He takes a deep breath and, with a howl and flash, changes himself into the god of wildfire. Roaring around like a huge flying bonfire, he burns up heaven and earth and, finally, even himself.

Holy Mistletoe
Mistletoe was holy to the Vikings because it grew on oak trees, which attracted Thor's thunderbolts (lightning). Celtic priests and priestesses also collected mistletoe, with golden sickles.

The End of the World
All ancient people were afraid the world would end violently. The Hebrews said it would happen in the battle of "Armageddon." The word, still used today, comes from Megiddo, a place in Israel where there had been many important battles in ancient times.

BEOWULF, *the* MONSTER-MASHER

THE DANISH KING'S HALL, packed with happy partygoers, rocked to the sound of singing, mead slurping, and table thumping. The din carried across the moors to the ears of Grendel, a fiend who screamed at even the thought of a smile. That night, he entered the hall, tore thirty snoring soldiers to pieces, and escaped into the fog.

This sort of thing went on for twelve years, until the king was at the end of his rope. Then Beowulf (*bay-oh-wolf*), hero of the Geat (*yay-at*) people, turned up with some friends to lend a hand. The king was delighted, but one of his soldiers, Unferth, sneered that anything a Geat could do, a Dane could do better. "We'll see about that," muttered Beowulf, and took his men off to the hall.

That night, Grendel smashed down the door, grabbed a Geat by the hair, and ate him feet first. Woken by the crunching, Beowulf jumped up and tackled the monster with his bare hands. Grendel had never met anyone so strong and tried to escape.

But Beowulf clung on to his arm until, with a horrible tearing sound, it ripped off, and Grendel ran away howling into the dark.

Special Swords
Many ancient peoples had special swords. The most famous Japanese sword was Kusanagi. The hero Sutano-woe found it in an eight-headed snake and gave it to his sister, the sun-goddess Amaterasu.

Even Unferth now agreed that Beowulf was no ordinary hero, and joined in the celebrations. However, the Danes' troubles were not over. The next night Grendel's mom, a stinking monster, came sniffing around the hall looking for revenge.

She killed a Dane before Beowulf woke up and launched into the mother of all fights. The monster scratched, bit, and clawed. Beowulf dodged, stabbed, and sliced with his sword. Blood and slime dripped onto the floor, bits of claw and metal flew into the air.

Heavenly Hall
Viking and Anglo-Saxon kings lived in large wooden halls. The Vikings believed fallen warriors spent their days feasting and drinking in the heavenly hall, Valhalla.

After a time, the monster chose home ground and ran back to her smelly cave at the bottom of a lake. Beowulf followed and, with the wounded Grendel shouting on the sidelines, began the second half of the fight. Beowulf's holy armor kept off the worst of the monster's attacks, but as he couldn't pierce her skin, he began to tire.

Just when he thought he was going to lose, he noticed a special giant-made sword gleaming in a corner. He grabbed it and, with one last effort, beheaded the monster and finished off Grendel. The sword blade fizzled away in the monsters' blood, leaving him with only the hilt as a souvenir.

Beowulf was so exhausted he barely made it back to the surface. News of what he'd done soon spread around and everyone agreed that, although he was a Geat, he was the greatest hero ever.

Lake Monsters
Tales of monsters have been told from Loch Ness to Australia. Before the Shushwap tribe of Washington went fishing in Lake Okanagan, they threw a chicken into the water to please the lake monster, Naitaka.

ROLAND *and the* SUPERHORN

THE KING OF THE FRANKS, Charlemagne (*shar-le-main*), had gone to Spain to enjoy a bit of Saracen smashing. But things went wrong and it was the Franks, not the Saracens, who got smashed. They were now crawling home through the mountains, with the Saracens hot on their heels.

If the Saracen horsemen caught them before they reached the plain, the Franks were done for. They had only a few miles to go, but it was hard work carrying all the sick and wounded. Charlemagne looked behind him and frowned. The cloud of dust thrown up by the enemy horsemen was getting closer every minute.

Charles the Great
Charlemagne, or Charles the Great (747–814), was a famous king of the Franks (early French). On Christmas Day 800 A.D., the pope crowned him Holy Roman Emperor.

He called Roland, his top knight, to his side. "It's up to you, Rolly. Take a band of volunteers and hold off the enemy until we're safely out of the mountains."

"Yes sir!" barked Roland. "No trouble, sir!"

"Thanks, Rolly." Charlemagne smiled. "And if you get into trouble, just blow your superhorn, Olifant. We'll hear it all right."

As the king and the rest of the army hobbled off to the plain, Roland lined up his men across the road in a narrow valley. Before long a band of fierce Saracens were upon them.

What a Whopper!
*The battle in this legend, Roncevaux (*ron-sir-voh*), took place in 778 A.D. Really there were just a few hundred people involved. But the legend says there were 400,000 men in the Saracen army – to make the Franks seem like brilliant fighters!*

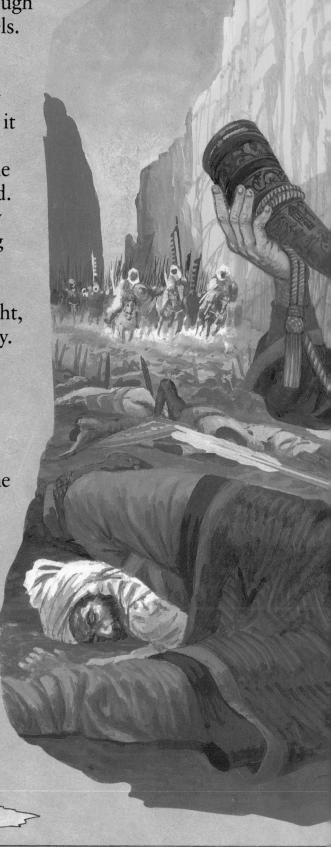

After a great deal of clashing and bashing, all the Saracens (and quite a few Franks) lay dead on the road. At that moment a second band of Saracens rode into view.

"Rats!" cried Roland's sergeant. "Not another bunch! Better blow your superhorn, Olifant, sir. We're going to need a bit of help with this group."

Roland frowned. "Help? Who needs help, sergeant? Do you think I'm soft!" He was a proud fellow as well as a brave one. As before, after a lot of clashing and bashing, all the Saracens (and quite a few Franks) lay dead on the road. When a third Saracen band came on the scene, the sergeant begged Roland to blow Olifant. Once again, the proud knight refused.

The third battle was even bloodier than the other two. Although Roland won, he now had almost no men left. So when a fourth Saracen band galloped up, he finally gave the horn a blow.

BLA-A-A-A-ARE! The sound of the superhorn bellowed through the mountains like an earthquake. At the deafening din, birds fell dead from the sky and Roland's horse collapsed. Far away, on the edge of the plain, Charlemagne heard the call and raced to the rescue.

He arrived to find a pile of bodies blocking the valley. The last Saracen attack had been driven off, but Roland and all his men were dead. Olifant, the superhorn, cracked from end to end, would never sound again.

Powerful Horns!
In medieval times, horns were signs of power.
They also made handy musical instruments
and drinking cups – but because of their shape they
could not be put down until they were empty!

BABUSHKA

ONE EVENING, EVERYONE in the village was outside staring up at the new star. Everyone except Babushka, that is. She was too busy cleaning her house. Since the death of her child, she hadn't been interested in anything else. All day, every day, she did nothing but wipe, scrub, polish, and sweep.

She was a bit annoyed, therefore, when three odd-looking foreign gentlemen knocked at her door and asked if they could spend the night. Nobody else seemed to be at home, they explained. Babushka frowned at their filthy shoes, but she had a kind heart and agreed to put them up.

The men's names were Gaspar, Melchior (*mell-key-or*), and Balthasar. Over dinner they explained that they were princes who were on their way to visit a baby king. They invited Babushka to go with them.

The invitation reminded her of her own son. She liked babies, too, and felt she could do with a break. On the other hand, she thought her house would get dirty if she went away. Besides, she didn't have a nice enough present for a king. So the next morning the princes climbed onto their camels and left without her.

Christmas Presents
The custom of giving Christmas presents goes back to Roman times, when gifts were handed out during the midwinter feast of the god Saturn. December 25th was not called Christmas Day until 900 years after Jesus Christ had died.

22

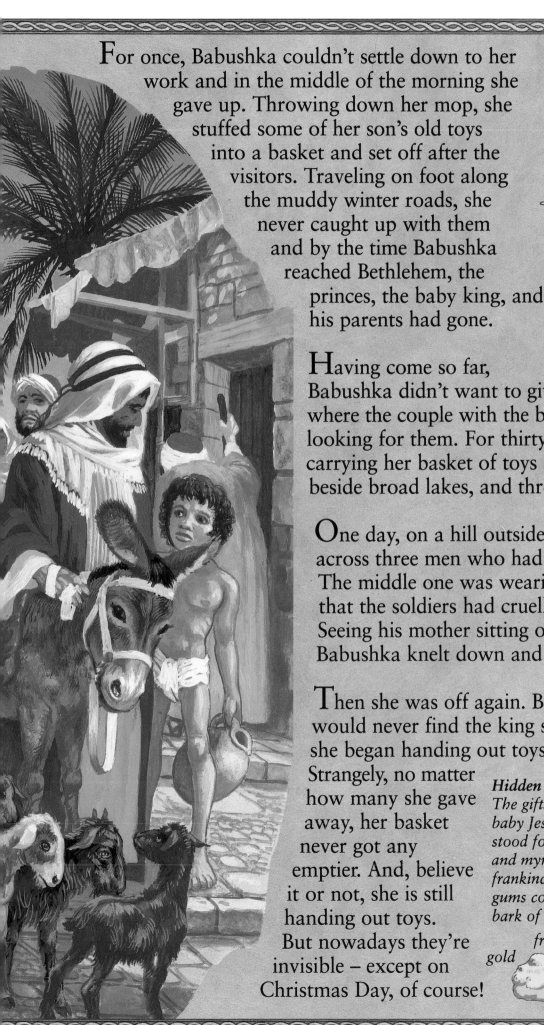

For once, Babushka couldn't settle down to her work and in the middle of the morning she gave up. Throwing down her mop, she stuffed some of her son's old toys into a basket and set off after the visitors. Traveling on foot along the muddy winter roads, she never caught up with them and by the time Babushka reached Bethlehem, the princes, the baby king, and his parents had gone.

We Three Kings
The three "kings" of the Christmas story were actually three wise men, or Magi. They were clever Persian priests who worshiped the god of fire.

Having come so far, Babushka didn't want to give up. She asked people where the couple with the baby had gone and began looking for them. For thirty years she traveled, carrying her basket of toys along dusty paths, beside broad lakes, and through bustling towns.

One day, on a hill outside Jerusalem, she came across three men who had been nailed to a cross. The middle one was wearing a crown of thorns that the soldiers had cruelly shoved onto his head. Seeing his mother sitting on the ground in tears, Babushka knelt down and comforted her.

Then she was off again. But now, realizing she would never find the king she was looking for, she began handing out toys to every child she met. Strangely, no matter how many she gave away, her basket never got any emptier. And, believe it or not, she is still handing out toys. But nowadays they're invisible – except on Christmas Day, of course!

Hidden Meanings
The gifts the Three Kings brought the baby Jesus had hidden meanings. Gold stood for royalty, frankincense for god, and myrrh for death. Myrrh and frankincense were both nice-smelling gums collected from the bark of special trees.

myrrh

frankincense

gold

The HOLY GRAIL

To show how holy they were, Christians used to collect special religious souvenirs. There were sacred skulls, loads of bones, piles of wood and cloth, and even a few saintly fingernails. But most precious of all was the Holy Grail. This was the cup that Jesus and his followers had drunk from during their last supper together.

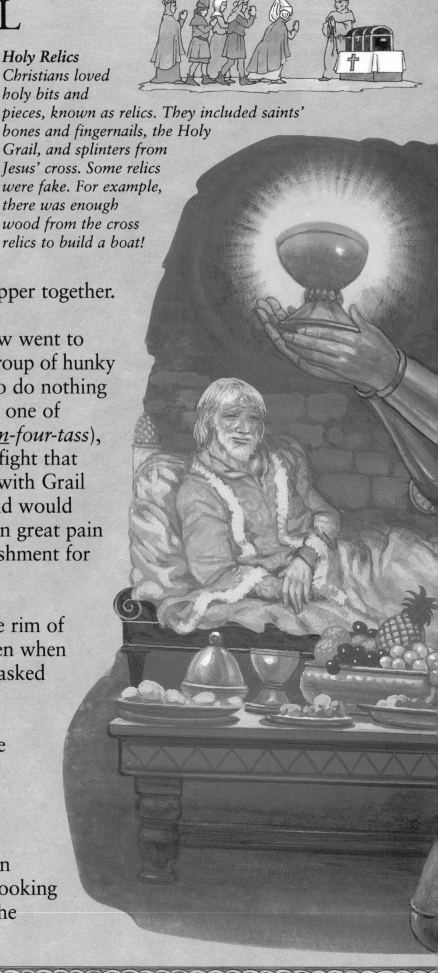

Holy Relics
Christians loved holy bits and pieces, known as relics. They included saints' bones and fingernails, the Holy Grail, and splinters from Jesus' cross. Some relics were fake. For example, there was enough wood from the cross relics to build a boat!

"This is My Blood"
During their last supper together, Jesus and his followers shared bread and wine. Jesus said the wine was his blood, so the cup they drank out of became very holy.

The Grail somehow went to England, where a group of hunky knights promised to do nothing but guard it. When one of them, Amfortas (*am-four-tass*), was wounded in a fight that had nothing to do with Grail guarding, his wound would not heal. He lived in great pain and misery as punishment for breaking his word.

One day, a message appeared on the rim of the Grail: Amfortas would be forgiven when a young man came to his castle and asked kindly what was wrong with him. Cheered by what he had read, the knight spent hours looking out of the window to see if a young lad was coming his way.

Eventually, a horseman did come trotting into view. He was Parsifal, an innocent but well-mannered knight looking for adventure. Amfortas welcomed the young man into the castle.

Then Amfortas showed the knight the Grail, and even allowed him to eat a magic meal that came out of it. But Parsifal didn't want to seem rude, so he never once asked his host why he was so miserable.

When Parsifal woke up the next morning, the castle was empty. He found his way out and set off to look for some adventure. He hadn't gone far when he bumped into a woman who explained about Amfortas and his wound. Realizing how stupid he had been, Parsifal dashed back the way he had come. But he was too late. The castle, the knights, everything had vanished.

Magic Medicine
In the Middle Ages, religion and magic were often mixed up. There were many stories of miracle cures, when people were made better through believing in God.

Feeling really guilty, Parsifal spent years looking for the castle and its Holy Grail. He had dozens of adventures with pretty maidens and rather less pretty villains. Finally, older and much wiser, he found himself back at Amfortas' castle again.

This time he was determined to do the right thing. He accepted Amfortas' hospitality and at the right moment, with angels singing in his ears, he gently asked him why he was in such pain.

Amfortas was cured immediately. A broad smile spread across his face, his eyes filled with tears of happiness, and even the Grail showed its joy by glowing with holy light. Parsifal's reward was to be invited to join the famous knights of the Holy Grail, a job that kept him busy for the rest of his days.

Joseph of Arimathea
Joseph of Arimathea was a Jew who believed in Jesus but didn't dare tell anyone. Legend says he went to Britain with the Holy Grail, set up an abbey at Glastonbury (right), *and began spreading the Christian message.*

JOAN of ARC

THIRTEEN-YEAR-OLD JOAN found religious studies homework really hard. One evening she took a break from prophets and parables and went into the garden for a breath of fresh air. As she was standing near the apple tree, she heard someone calling her name.

Looking up, she saw three ghostly shapes floating over the gooseberry bushes. "Who are you? What do you want?" she asked, wishing she had stayed indoors.

"I'm Saint Michael," said one of the shapes. Goose pimples appeared all over Joan's body. "I'm Saint Catherine," said the second shape. "And I'm Saint Margaret," added the third. "Now listen carefully!" they all said together. "You will shove the enemy out of France."

Strange Visions
In the Middle Ages, "visions" were often no more than dreams. Perhaps Joan just dreamed she saw three saints in her garden?

"E-enemy?" stuttered Joan, shaking like a wet dog. "You mean the English?" "Yeah!" answered the shapes. "God's chosen you to save France! Good luck!" As the saints had nothing more to add, Joan went inside to finish her homework.

Two days later, she told a soldier what had happened. As only really holy people see visions, he thought she was mad, or even a witch, so he got a priest to check her out. When the priest said she was OK, the soldier took her to meet the French prince.

Hundred Years of War
The story of Joan of Arc comes from the time when England and France were at war for 100 years. Not long after Joan's victories, the French finally won.

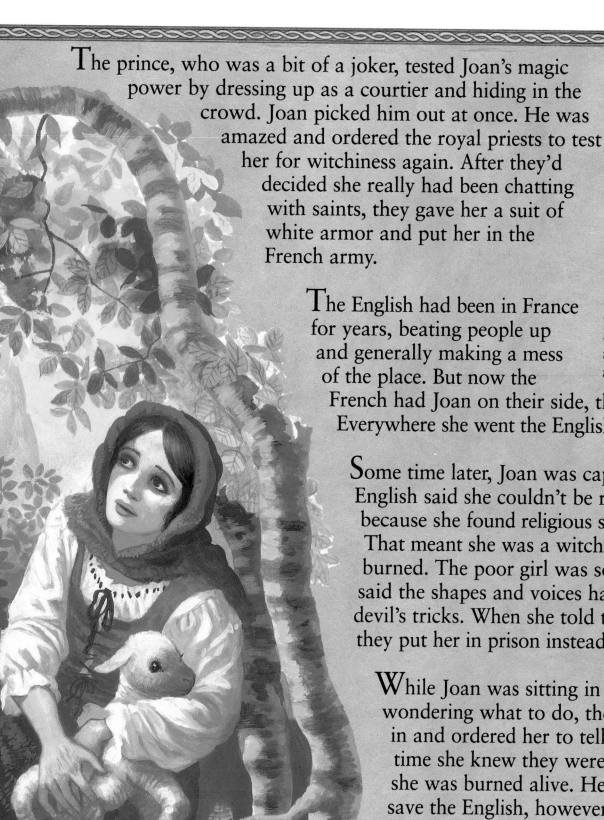

The prince, who was a bit of a joker, tested Joan's magic power by dressing up as a courtier and hiding in the crowd. Joan picked him out at once. He was amazed and ordered the royal priests to test her for witchiness again. After they'd decided she really had been chatting with saints, they gave her a suit of white armor and put her in the French army.

The English had been in France for years, beating people up and generally making a mess of the place. But now the French had Joan on their side, things changed. Everywhere she went the English were defeated.

Some time later, Joan was captured. The English said she couldn't be really holy because she found religious studies difficult. That meant she was a witch and had to be burned. The poor girl was so terrified she said the shapes and voices had been the devil's tricks. When she told the English this, they put her in prison instead of burning her.

While Joan was sitting in her cell wondering what to do, the saints floated in and ordered her to tell the truth. This time she knew they were for real and she was burned alive. Her death didn't save the English, however, and they were soon driven from France. Afterward, as a way of saying thanks, the French made Joan a saint.

Good or Evil?
Witches' "spells" were usually just the innocent mutterings of old women and their "magic potions" were often natural medicines.

Burn Her!
Witches were burned to save their souls. Priests believed their wickedness would be removed by fire.

BABA YAGA

BABA YAGA WAS THE MOST disgusting, horrible, stinking, foul witch in all of Russia. She was thin and pointed, with a jutting jaw, spider's legs, and needle fingers. When she opened her mouth to eat a freshly boiled child, her iron teeth made her look like a ferocious monster.

Ghastly Grannies? Real "witches" were often just lonely or sick old women. Because they were weak, it was easy to pick on them.

Everyone knew this and kept out of Baba's way. But no one knew she had a sister, Biba Yaga. Biba didn't eat children herself, but she supplied juicy young girls for her sister's pantry. This brings us to Misha Poltoy, a pretty girl who lived with her father on the edge of town.

One spring, Mr. Poltoy got married again. His new wife was mean and harsh. In case you hadn't guessed, she was Biba Yaga, and she had married Mr. Poltoy just to get at Misha.

Soon after the wedding, when Mr. Poltoy was at work, Biba told Misha to go to a woman in the forest to borrow some knitting needles. Off the girl went, taking a loaf of bread and cold meat for lunch. She felt a bit nervous as soon as she met the stranger, and when she saw her steely teeth she screamed in horror. She had walked straight into the den of Baba Yaga!

Leaving Misha in the kitchen, guarded by a huge black dog and a mean-looking cat, the witch went to draw a bath. She always scrubbed her victims clean before eating them.

Misha turned to the animals. "Please help me!" she begged.

"What's in it for us?" they asked. Misha looked at their thin sides and mangy coats. "Food! I'll give you bread and meat if you help."

The starving animals jumped at the idea. As Misha handed over her lunch, they gave her a magic towel and a comb. "Run for your life!" they said. "When Baba has almost caught you, throw the towel down behind you. And when she's about to grab you again, drop the comb. Now scram!"

As she ran, Misha heard the witch screeching and following after her in a huge cooking pot. Just in time, she dropped the towel and the comb as the animals said. The towel turned into a wide river. Baba's pot sank and she had to swim across. The comb grew into a forest so thick that the witch got lost and gave up the chase.

When Misha got home and told her father about Biba, he threw the woman out. They never saw the evil sisters again. But Baba was always hungry, and many young girls were not as lucky as Misha.

The Wild Wood
Much of northwest Europe was once covered with thick woodland. As a result, the region's myths and legends are full of dark forests and wild, dangerous woods.

Black Cats
In Christian myth, when the devil turned himself into an animal, his favorite choice was a cat. That's why witches were often thought to live with a black cat.

ROMEO *and* JULIET

AT FIRST GLANCE, the Italian city of Verona was a great place. The sun shone, there was no plague, and the merchants were fat and rich. But all was definitely not well. The two most important families, the Montagues (<u>mon</u>-ta-gyoos) and Capulets (<u>cap</u>-you-lets), hated each other's guts, which gave the city a really nasty atmosphere.

Modern Romeos
Shakespeare's play Romeo and Juliet *made the story famous, and today all young lover-boys are called Romeos. But, strangely, their lovers are not called Juliets!*

The stupid thing was, on their own, the Montagues and Capulets were decent people. But put them together and… KER-POW! So when Lord Montague's son, Romeo, went to a Capulet dress up party, he was asking for trouble.

And trouble came, too, because he and Lord Capulet's daughter Juliet met and fell head over heels in love.

The starry-eyed teenage lovers met in secret and decided to get married, whatever their families might say. But luck was not on their side. Romeo, who was a clever swordsman, got mixed up in a street fight and was banished from the city for killing a man.

As if this wasn't bad enough for Juliet, her dad told her she had to marry a fellow named Count Paris. He was OK, but she didn't like him one bit.

Family vs. Family
There were rival gangs, like the Montagues and Capulets, in many Italian cities. The Guelphs (<u>gwelfs</u>) and Ghibellines (<u>gib</u>-uh-leans) of Milan hated each other so much that they had different ways of walking, talking, sneezing, and even cutting fruit!

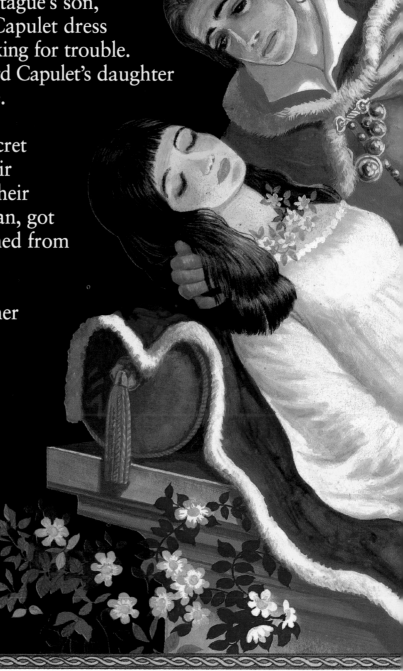

Juliet explained her problem to a friendly priest. The crafty fellow advised her to agree to marry Paris but also to take a special drug. This would make her look as if she'd died, and her wedding to Paris would be called off.

The priest sent a message to Romeo explaining that, whatever he heard, Juliet was not really dead. He should sneak into her tomb and carry her off. Then, if everything worked out all right, when the drug wore off they could live happily ever after.

Mini-Marriage
In Europe it used to be quite common for rich and powerful families to arrange marriages between children, who had no say in the matter.

But things didn't work out – the priest's message didn't get through. Crazy with unhappiness, Romeo went to have one last look at Juliet in her tomb. There he met Paris and killed him. Because he had nothing left to live for, he put an end to his misery by taking poison.

What had begun as a love story was now looking more like a horror movie. To make things worse, at this point Juliet woke up. Seeing her beloved Romeo dead, with the empty bottle of poison beside him, she realized what had happened. All her hopes and dreams were shattered, so she stabbed herself.

The rest of the Montagues and Capulets now turned up at the tomb. Looking around at the mess, it finally dawned on them that none of this would have happened if they'd gotten along better. So, better late than never, they shook hands and made up.

Doomed Lovers
There are many stories of tragic lovers from around the world. Greece's most famous pair were Hero and Leander. Every night, Leander swam across a broad stretch of sea to be with his beloved Hero. But one night he drowned and she jumped into the water to die with him.

DON QUIXOTE
and the WINDMILLS

DON QUIXOTE (*key-oh-tea*) OF LA MANCHA, Spain, was old and broke. He lived in the past, dreaming of the time when knights in armor went around killing dragons and rescuing ladies in distress from castle towers. He was so taken up with these romantic tales that he decided to go off on a hairbrained adventure of his own.

First, he put on his armor, not noticing that it was rusty and battered. Then, armed with a rotted lance and a borrowed sword, he clambered onto the back of his trusty Rosinante (*ros-ee-nan-tay*), a horse who was just about as worn out as he was. Finally, he got a local farmworker, Sancho Panza, to come along with him as his squire.

Blown Away
The story of Don Quixote was written at a time when the invention of guns meant that armored knights no longer ruled the battlefield. But today, it is still an honor to be made a knight and called "sir."

Don Quixote had read in storybooks that knights always did their valiant deeds to show off to the ladies. Unfortunately, there weren't any noble maidens who fancied Don Quixote, so he said he was fighting for the heart of Dulcinea, a pretty girl from the next village. Luckily, she didn't know about this.

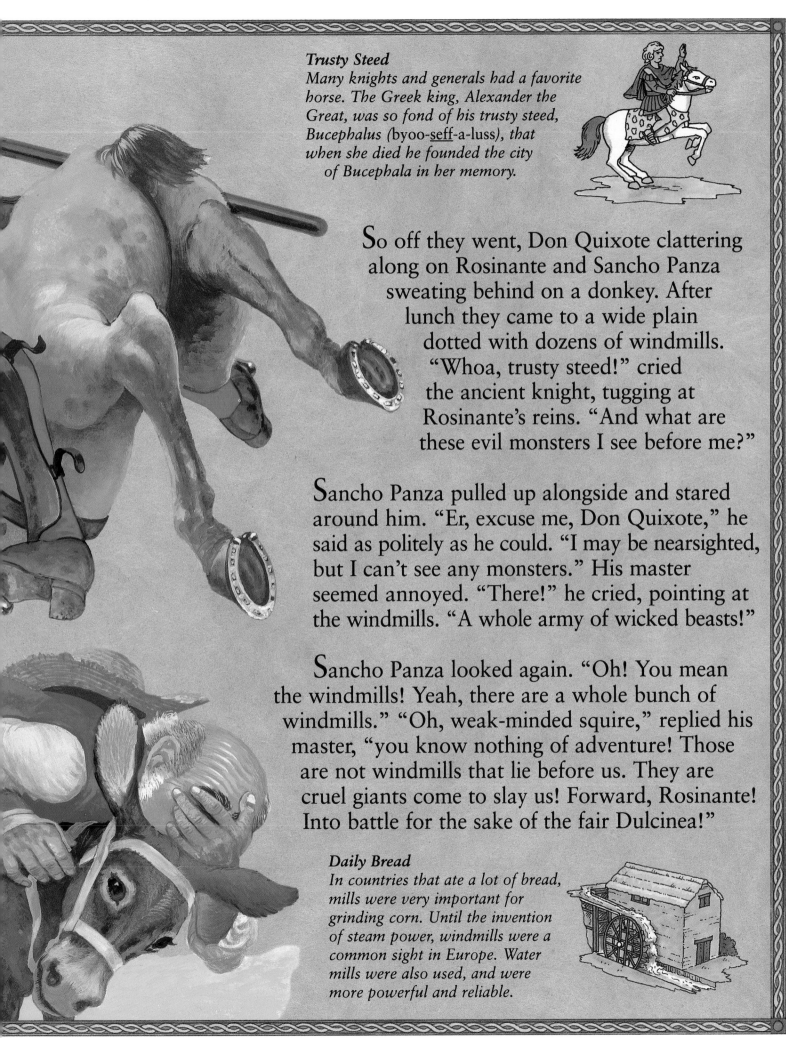

Trusty Steed
Many knights and generals had a favorite horse. The Greek king, Alexander the Great, was so fond of his trusty steed, Bucephalus (byoo-<u>seff</u>-a-luss), that when she died he founded the city of Bucephala in her memory.

So off they went, Don Quixote clattering along on Rosinante and Sancho Panza sweating behind on a donkey. After lunch they came to a wide plain dotted with dozens of windmills. "Whoa, trusty steed!" cried the ancient knight, tugging at Rosinante's reins. "And what are these evil monsters I see before me?"

Sancho Panza pulled up alongside and stared around him. "Er, excuse me, Don Quixote," he said as politely as he could. "I may be nearsighted, but I can't see any monsters." His master seemed annoyed. "There!" he cried, pointing at the windmills. "A whole army of wicked beasts!"

Sancho Panza looked again. "Oh! You mean the windmills! Yeah, there are a whole bunch of windmills." "Oh, weak-minded squire," replied his master, "you know nothing of adventure! Those are not windmills that lie before us. They are cruel giants come to slay us! Forward, Rosinante! Into battle for the sake of the fair Dulcinea!"

Daily Bread
In countries that ate a lot of bread, mills were very important for grinding corn. Until the invention of steam power, windmills were a common sight in Europe. Water mills were also used, and were more powerful and reliable.

With these words, Don Quixote lowered his lance, urged Rosinante into a trot, and, yelling weird war cries, charged straight at the windmills. Sancho Panza scratched his head and watched to see what would happen.

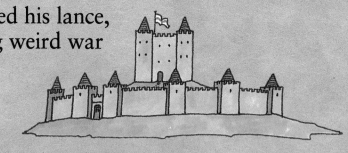

While the crazy old man was still some way off his target, a breeze came up. The sails of the windmills creaked and slowly started to turn. Don Quixote shouted that the giants had seen him coming and were waving their weapons at him. He persuaded Rosinante to canter and headed for the nearest windmill.

The End of Castles
In another of his adventures, Don Quixote stopped at a wayside inn and thought it was a castle. In fact, only the mightiest families had a castle of their own. And, like knights, castles also became less important when cannons were invented that could blow them up.

When he reached it, his lance went straight through the canvas sail and got stuck. He was so excited he forgot to let go. The flapping sail lifted him right out of the saddle before his lance broke, and he crashed to the ground in a heap. Sancho Panza took a deep breath and helped his master to his feet. "I told you they weren't giants," he grumbled.

Doing a Favor
Ladies tied a scarf – called a favor – around the lance of their favorite knight. This was to remind him of her when he was fighting.

Don Quixote, shaken but unharmed, stared at him in amazement. "Not giants?" he cried. "Oh, Panza! My dear Panza! Do you still not understand? Of course they were giants. But just as I was going to slay them, the wicked magician Freston changed them into windmills. Imagine you not realizing that!"

Sancho Panza shrugged. "Oh, well, if you say they were giants, I suppose they were giants. You're the master." Don Quixote smiled. "Of course, Panza. Now you see the sort of evil we are up against." Panza was not sure that he did, but he helped the knight back into the saddle, and the two of them rode off in search of more adventures.

Handy Helper
No knight was complete without his squire to help him put on his armor and mount his horse.

TRICKY TERMS

All words in italics, e.g. *souls*, have their own explanation.

Devil
The Vikings and Celts believed in a world with many gods and goddesses. The Christians, however, introduced the idea of a single, male God. His rival was the Devil, who stood for all that was evil.

Heaven
The home of gods, goddesses, and the *souls* of people who have led good lives. The Viking heaven was called Asgard, and the Celts called the resting place of *spirits* the "Otherworld," found in the West.

Immortal
A living thing that can never die or be killed.

Legend
A story that has grown up around a heroic figure (who may have been a real person) or event (that may have actually taken place).

Mead
An alcoholic drink made from honey and water that was popular with the Vikings and Celts.

Prophet or **Prophetess**
Someone who foretells the future.

Ritual
A set of holy actions that form part of religious worship. Many important events in our lives, such as birth, marriage, and death, are marked by rituals.

Sacred
The most important parts of religion, or anything that is holy.

Sacrifice
A ritual offering to a god or goddess to thank them for their help, or to ask for their support. In the ancient world, the gift was often a human or animal victim.

Soul
The part of a creature that thinks and feels. Ancient peoples believed that the soul was *immortal*, and that when a person or creature died, their soul went to *heaven*.

Spirit
A living being that has no body. Spirit can also mean the *soul* of a creature.

Valhalla
The Vikings believed that slain warriors went to this hall in *heaven*, to prepare for the final battle against the forces of evil. Its walls were made of shields and its roof of swords.

WHO'S WHO

A guide to the hottest names in Viking, Celtic, and Middle-Age myths and legends. Names in capitals, e.g. KING ARTHUR, have their own explanation.

Aegir (_eye_-gear)
The salty Viking god of the sea, whose nine daughters were thought to move the waves. He and his wife, Ran, caught sailors with a net, and dragged them down to the hall in their deep-sea kingdom.

Arthur (_ar_-thur)
Arthur (*top*) was a legendary king of the Celts. The real Arthur probably battled against Anglo-Saxon invaders in the early 6th century A.D. He pops up in many legends of the

Viking hall

Middle Ages, which tell of his court at Camelot and his queen, Guinevere (_gwin-uh-veer_). Arthur was also famous for his magic sword, Excalibur, and for creating the Knights of the Round Table. They include Lancelot (_lan_-sell-lot), GALAHAD (_gal_-a-had), and GAWAIN (_gah-wain_). The knights had many adventures fighting for truth, justice, and the Christian way. However, in the end, Arthur's nephew, Mordred, rebelled against the king, and in a huge battle most of Arthur's knights were killed. The dying king was taken in a ship by three fairies to the magical island of Avalon – where he is still said to be sleeping.

Asgard (_as_-gard)
Asgard was home to the Viking gods. A mighty fortress, it was surrounded by a wall and joined to MIDGARD (the earth), by the rainbow bridge, Bifrost. Each god and goddess had a hall of their own, while dead warriors feasted and fought in Valhalla.

Domovoi

Balder (_bal_-dur)
The handsome Viking sun god Balder stood for goodness and wisdom. He died when the evil LOKI tricked the sun god's blind brother into hurling a mistletoe dart at him – the only thing that could kill Balder.

Barbarossa (_bar-bar-ross-ah_)
Named "Barbarossa" after his bushy red beard, Frederick I was a real king who ruled over much of Germany and Italy in the 12th century A.D. But after his death, people said that he was just taking a nap under a hill, and would return when Germany needed him most.

Beowulf (_bay_-oh-wolf)
Beowulf was the legendary prince of the Geats (_yay-ats_), a Viking tribe from what is now southern Sweden. After killing the monstrous Grendel and his mother, he ruled for 50 peaceful years. When a dragon started to bully his people, the aged Beowulf killed it, but died after breathing in its poisonous fumes.

Bragi (_brag_-ee)
The Viking god of poetry and knowledge. He welcomed slain warriors to Valhalla by singing jolly songs to them.

Bran (_bran_)
A legendary king of the Celts. In British myth, the giant Bran ordered his followers to cut off his head when he died. They are said to have buried it at the White Mount, later the site of the Tower of London. In Irish legend, Bran sailed to a magical place called the Otherworld.

Brighid (_bridge_-it)
The Celtic goddess of poetry, healing, and metalwork.

Brunhild (_brun_-_hilld_)
The leader of the VALKYRIES.

Charlemagne (_shar_-le-_main_)
Charlemagne (742–814 A.D.) was King of the Franks. But, as with BARBAROSSA, legends grew up around the real person. One said that he never died – he is just snoozing with his knights under a mountain, ready to wake when France is in danger.

Cuchulain (coo-_kull_-in)
The greatest of the Irish heroes, Cuchulain was a shocking sight in battle – one eye bulged, the other sank into his skull, and his hair stood up and caught on fire! His "salmon leap" allowed him to jump over any obstacle, and his favorite weapon was a magic spear.

Dagda (_dag_-dah)
The Celtic god of life and death, who controlled the weather (_left_). He looked like an old peasant with a fat belly. He also owned a cauldron that never ran out of food, however much you took out of it.

The Devil

Domovoi (_dom_-oh-voy)
The mythical spirits of the home of the Slavs (the peoples of eastern Europe). Covered in silky hair, they came out at night (_center, page 36_). Food was often left out for them, to bring good luck.

Druids (_drew_-ids)
The sacred priests and teachers of the Celts, who worshiped the god DAGDA in particular.

Dvergar (de-_ver_-gar)
These very short but stocky men were created by the Viking gods. They were thought to live in mountains and caves, and were famed for their skill in metalwork. Though they were usually kind, they killed anyone who stole their treasure.

El Cid (_ell sid_)
In legend, Spain's Christian hero, El Cid, was greatly feared by the Muslim Saracens. After he died, Christians were said to have tied his body to a horse to make him seem immortal. The real man, called Ruy Diàz de Bivar, lived in the 11th century A.D. and fought both Christians and Muslims.

Fenrir (_fen_-rear)
Fenrir was the wolf monster son of LOKI. When he roared, his lower jaw grazed the earth and his nose lifted up to heaven. He became so fierce the gods decided to tie him up. Only TYR managed this. He used a magic chain made from the sinew of a bear, the breath of a fish, the root of a mountain, the beard of a woman, the sound of a cat's step, and the saliva of a bird.

Finn Mac Cool (*fin ma-cool*)

Another great fighter who was said to be not dead but merely having a rest in a cave, Irish hero Finn Mac Cool was the leader of a band of warriors, the Fianna. As a boy (*top*), Finn ate the Salmon of Knowledge. After this, if he ever needed to know anything, he stuck his thumb in his mouth and sang special words!

Frey (*fray*)
The Viking god of plenty, Frey owned a ship that could carry all the gods – but could also be folded into a tiny parcel when not in use.

Freya (*fray-ya*)
The Viking goddess of good harvests and love, and sister of FREY. She wore the beautiful necklace Brisingamen (*bry-sing-amen*), which she won from the DVERGAR.

Frigg (*frig*)
The Viking goddess of childbirth and the wife of ODIN.

Galahad (*gal-a-had*)
The purest and most noble of ARTHUR's Knights of the Round Table.

Gawain (*gah-wain*)
In one Middle Age's legend, a giant Green Knight challenged any knights of the Round Table to cut off his head or lose their own head in a year's time. Gawain bravely accepted. But when the Green Knight was beheaded, he picked up his head and rode off! A year later, Gawain offered his head, but his life was spared as he was noble enough to keep his word.

Saint George
George was famed for killing a fiery dragon. In 303 A.D., the real George was executed by the Romans for being a Christian.

Heimdall (*haym-dahl*)
In Viking myth, Heimdall watched over the rainbow bridge to warn the gods if the giants were about to attack.

Hel (*hell*)
The Viking goddess of the dead, who lived in NIFLHEIM.

Jotnar (*yurt-nar*)
The Vikings believed the jotnar, or giants, were the enemies of the gods and would defeat them at RAGNAROK, the final battle.

Thor's hammer

Kikimora (*key-key-more-ah*)
Female spirits of the home in Russian mythology, thought to be small with long hair.

Loki (*lock-ee*)
The Viking trickster god, who sometimes played jokes on the other gods, but also helped them. His main skills were changing shape and his light fingers, which allowed him to steal FREYA's necklace and the Apples of Youth. But at RAGNAROK, it is Loki who destroys the world.

Midgard (*mid-gard*)
The Viking word for earth, or the world of humans. This lies midway between ASGARD (home of the gods), and the home of the giants.

William Tell

Morgan Le Fay
The half-sister and enemy of Arthur. A witch, she had magical healing powers and could fly. She trapped Merlin (*left*) with a spell. Her son Mordred led the rebellion against KING ARTHUR and the Knights of the Round Table.

Niflheim (*nif-ul-haym*)
The Viking land of the dead, a world of mist, ice, and darkness.

Njord (*nyurd*)
The Viking god of the wind. His wife, Skadi, was a keen huntress. Sadly, they lived apart since he loved the sea while she could not bear to leave the forest.

Odin (*oh-din*)
The chief of the Viking gods, he was also god of battle, magic, and wisdom. He had only one eye, since he gave one up for a drink from the giant's Spring of Knowledge. He rode an eight-legged horse, Sleipnir (*slayp-neer*).

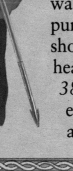

Robin Hood

Saint Patrick
In legend, this Irish saint drove all the snakes in Ireland into the sea. The real Patrick lived in the 5th century A.D. At 16, he was kidnapped by pirates and made into a slave. He escaped to Britain where he became a Christian monk.

Ragnarok (*rag-na-rurk*)
The final battle at the end of the world, to be fought between the gods and the giants.

Siegfried (*seeg-freed*)
A German hero of incredible strength. After he killed a dragon, its blood made him invincible except for one spot on his back where a leaf had fallen. After many adventures, he finally died when his wife was tricked into showing where his weak spot was.

William Tell
In Swiss legend, the 14th-century William Tell refused to obey the Austrian lord who was in charge of his town. As punishment, he was forced to shoot an apple off his son's head with a crossbow (*page 38*). This he did, and he later encouraged the Swiss to rebel against their foreign rulers.

Thor (*thor*)
Thor was the Viking thunder god. His hammer, Mjolnir (*page 38*), returned to his hand whenever he threw it.

Tyr (*teer*)
Tyr was the Viking god of war, who had his left hand bitten off when he tied up FENRIR with a magic chain.

Valkyries (*val-ki-rees*)
These warrior women chose who died in battle. They rode on horses through the sky to bring dead Vikings to Valhalla (*below*).

Werewolves
In European myth, werewolves were humans that changed into wolves during a full moon (*top*).

Wayland (*way-land*)
The king of the elves in German mythology, famous for his amazing metalwork. When captured by the king of the Swedes, he escaped using wings made from swans' feathers.

Yggdrasil (*igg-drah-sill*)
The Viking world tree. Of its three roots, one reached to ASGARD, one to NIFLHEIM, and a third to the land of the giants.

INDEX

The main stories for each name have page numbers in bold.